Pirates

Catriona Clarke

Designed by Laura Parker

Illustrated by
Terry McKenna

Pirate consultant: Dr. David Cordingly

Reading consultant: Alison Kelly, Roehampton University

Contents

Who were pirates?

Pirates were robbers who roamed the seas and stole from other ships.

This picture shows a pirate captain. His men are burying treasure.

The Golden Age

Three hundred years ago, thousands of pirates sailed the seas. This is called the Golden Age of Piracy.

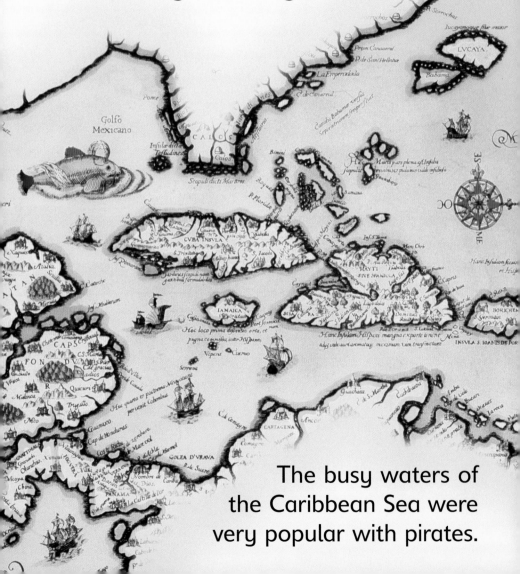

The busy waters of the Caribbean Sea were very popular with pirates.

Men became pirates for all kinds of reasons.

Some thought the life of a pirate would be full of adventure.

Lots of men thought they would be able to steal precious treasure.

A few expected an easy life with lots to eat and drink.

The pirate code

Every pirate had to agree to a strict set of rules at the start of each voyage.

Pirates had to keep their weapons clean and ready for action.

Every pirate had to fight bravely in times of battle.

The pirates were not allowed to fight each other on board ship.

On some ships, lights had to be out by eight o'clock at night.

Pirates settled their arguments
by having a duel on land.

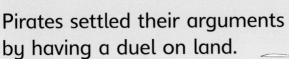

Pirates who did not obey
the code were punished.

One of the worst
punishments was
called marooning.

A pirate would be left without food on
a desert island. If he could not find food,
he would die.

A pirate ship

Some pirate ships were huge ships with three masts, but most were small, fast ships called sloops.

This is what a sloop looked like. A ship this size could carry up to 70 pirates.

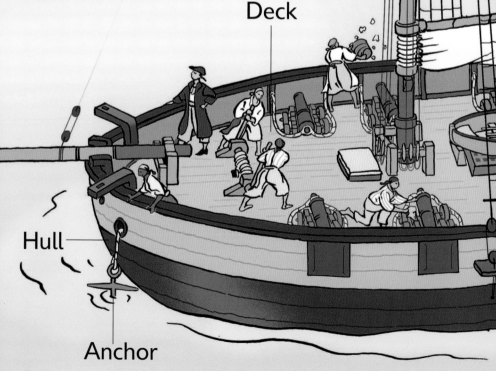

Mast

Deck

Hull

Anchor

Pirate captains were sometimes in charge of a group of ships - not just one.

Tiller for steering the sloop

Cannon Sail

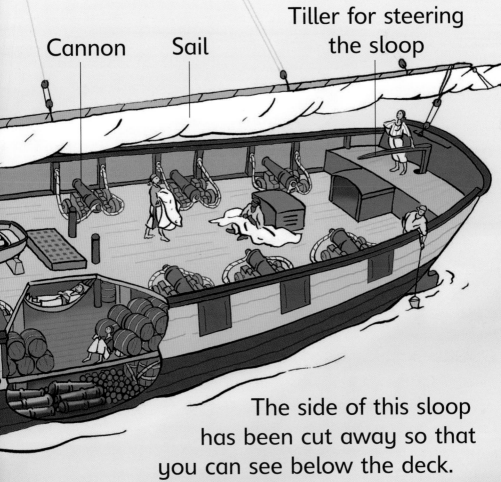

The side of this sloop has been cut away so that you can see below the deck.

Meet the crew

The captain was leader of the ship. He was chosen by the crew.

This is Billy Bones, a captain from a famous story called Treasure Island.

Sometimes the captain even had to share his cabin.

The quartermaster punished any pirates who broke the rules of the pirate code.

The helmsman steered the pirate ship using a long wooden tiller.

The cook was often a pirate who had been injured and could no longer fight.

Life at sea

A pirate's life wasn't as busy as a normal sailor's life. Pirates spent more of their time enjoying themselves.

Many pirates spent a lot of time eating and drinking.

They enjoyed singing songs called shanties, and dancing, too.

Pirates sometimes ate their biscuits in the dark so they couldn't see the bugs in them.

There were still jobs
to do, though.

The lookout watched
for other ships.

The sails had
to be hauled
up or down.

The deck
had to be
scrubbed
every day.

13

What to wear

Pirates mostly wore rough, plain clothes, but some wore fine clothes that they had stolen.

Captains often dressed like rich gentlemen.

This picture shows Captain Kidd, a famous pirate.

Pirates wore hats and headscarves to protect them from the hot sun.

They sometimes hung their pistols on fancy ribbons around their necks.

Pirates had short cutlasses which were good for fighting in tight spaces.

They liked to dress in their best clothes when they weren't at sea.

Attack!

The ships that pirates captured were called prizes. Most prizes surrendered quickly.

1. When pirates spotted a ship, they raised a flag called the Jolly Roger.

2. They chased the ship, firing their guns, until they caught up with it.

3. The pirates boarded the ship and began to search for treasure.

4. The quartermaster asked if any of the crew wanted to join the pirates.

Sometimes the ship's crew didn't give in so easily. This old painting shows a fierce battle.

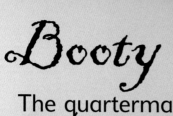

Booty

The quartermaster was in charge of the booty taken from a prize. He shared it out among the crew.

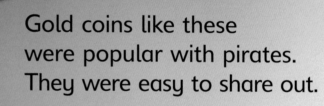

Gold coins like these were popular with pirates. They were easy to share out.

Men who were injured in a battle got a bigger share of the booty.

Gold, silver and jewels were the most precious kinds of booty.

Pirates also took useful things like tools, sails, clothes and food.

They often kept the prize itself and set the crew adrift on a small boat.

Land ahoy!

Pirates didn't spend all of their time at sea. They had to go ashore every few months to clean their ship. This was called careening.

1. The ship's hull became clogged with weeds and barnacles.

2. This made the ship move too slowly in the water.

3. The pirates had to beach the ship and tip it onto its side.

4. They scraped the hull clean and then coated it with tar.

The rest of the pirates relaxed and enjoyed themselves while the ship was being careened.

Pirates were often captured by the Navy while careening their ships.

Famous pirates

A few pirate captains were very well known.

Bartholomew Roberts was the most successful pirate. He captured more than 400 prizes before the Navy caught him.

Edward Low was one of the cruellest pirate captains of the Golden Age. He tortured the captains of the ships he attacked.

The most famous pirate was Blackbeard.
His real name was Edward Teach.

This old
painting shows
Blackbeard's
last battle.

Blackbeard stuck lighted
matches under his hat.
This made him look scary.

Women in disguise

Pirate rules did not allow women on board the ship, but women pirates did exist.

This old print shows Mary Read and Anne Bonny.

They were the most famous women pirates.

Mary and Anne dressed as men to disguise themselves.

They both joined the crew of a captain called Calico Jack.

They fought as fiercely as the men in lots of battles.

Mary and Anne were captured in 1720 with the rest of the crew.

Mary died in prison, but no one knows what happened to Anne.

End of an era

There were so many pirate attacks that the British Navy had to take action.

Big warships hunted down pirates and captured them.

The pirates were put on trial. Lots of people came to watch the trials.

If the pirates were found guilty at the trial, they were hanged.

Dead pirates were put in special cages like this one, so that everyone could see that being a pirate was a bad idea.

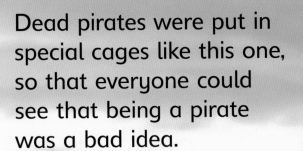

Each cage was specially made to fit each pirate.

The Golden Age ended when lots of pirates were captured and killed.

Beneath the waves

People have been searching for the wrecks of pirate ships since the Golden Age of Piracy.

The Whydah Galley sank in a terrible storm off the coast of Massachusetts, USA, in 1717.

In 1984, treasure hunters used a machine to detect the metal in the ship's cannons.

Divers found pieces of the ship and thousands of other treasures in the sand.

This pistol was one of the
many treasures found
with the wreck of the
Whydah Galley.

These bullets were
found inside the
barrel of the pistol.

Treasure hunters believe that
there is still lots of pirate
treasure that hasn't
been discovered yet.

Glossary of pirate words

Here are some of the words in this book you might not know. This page tells you what they mean.

 duel - a fight between two people to settle an argument.

 sloop - a small, fast ship. Lots of pirates sailed on sloops.

 tiller - a handle used to steer a ship. The tiller is attached to a rudder.

 cutlass - a short sword. Cutlasses were useful for fighting in tight spaces.

 Jolly Roger - a flag that pirates put up when they attacked another ship.

 booty - pirate treasure. Gold, silver and jewels were all types of booty.

 careen - to tip a ship on its side. This was done to repair and clean the hull.

Websites to visit

You can visit exciting websites to find out more about pirates.

To visit these websites, go to the Usborne Quicklinks Website at **www.usborne-quicklinks.com**
Read the internet safety guidelines, and then type the keywords "**beginners pirates**".

The websites are regularly reviewed and the links in Usborne Quicklinks are updated. However, Usborne Publishing is not responsible, and does not accept liability, for the content or availability of any website other than its own. We recommend that children are supervised while on the internet.

This ring and Spanish coin are treasures from the shipwreck of the Whydah Galley.

Index

Acknowledgements

The pictures on pages 3, 7 and 14 were painted by an artist called **Howard Pyle**. He painted lots of pirate pictures in the early twentieth century.

Photographic manipulation by John Russell

Photo credits

The publishers are grateful to the following for permission to reproduce material:
© Art media/Heritage-Images 16-17; © Atwater Kent Museum of Philadelphia/The Bridgeman Art Library 27;
© Bettman/CORBIS 23; © Blue Lantern Studio/CORBIS 2-3; © The Bridgeman Art Library 4-5;
© Delaware Art Museum, Wilmington, USA/The Bridgeman Art Library 7; © Digital Vision 1;
© Getty Images 1 (Ian McKinnell); © National Geographic Images Collection 18, 29 (Bill Curtsinger);
© Richard T. Nowitz/CORBIS 31; © Mary Evans Picture Library 10, 14;
© By kind permission of Mrs Susan M. Russell Flint/The Bridgeman Art Library 21.

Every effort has been made to trace and acknowledge ownership of copyright. If any rights have been omitted, the publishers offer to rectify this in any subsequent editions following notification.

 Sun, moon and stars

 Farm animals

 Elizabeth I

 Rubbish & Recycling

 Dogs

 Horses and ponies

 Spiders

 Planes

 Cats

 Ancient Greeks

 VOLCANOES

 Dinosaurs

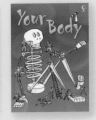 Your Body

 Armour

 Sharks

 The Celts

 VIKINGS

 Castles

 How flowers grow

 Digging up the past

 Living in space

 Caterpillars and Butterflies

 Ballet

 Pirates

 EGYPTIANS

Eggs and Chicks

ROMANS

Weather

Tadpoles and frogs

Why do we eat?

Under the sea

Bears

AZTECS

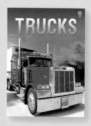
TRUCKS

Night Animals

Firefighters

Antarctica

Bugs

COWBOYS

Planet Earth

London

Seashore

China

Dangerous Animals

Rainforests

Trees

Reptiles

Ships

Bats

Penguins